BRONC TO BREAKFAST

& other poems by Mike Logan

illustrations by Mike Korn

BRONC TO BREAKFAST

& *other poems*

MIKE LOGAN

Bronc to Breakfast; watercolor by
Charlie Russell, courtesy Mackay Collection,
Montana Historical Society.

Published by Buglin' Bull Press

Library of Congress Catalog Card Number: 88-91264
ISBN 978-1-931832-91-5

Buglin' Bull Press

Dedication

This book is dedicated to my sons,
Mark and Sean,
who shared my camps and made
all my trails happy ones.

Foreword

I have a suspicion that there are about twelve Wilson trailer loads of "cowboy" or "western" poets clattering around the countryside. Each poet has a boot box half full of poems. If you unloaded them all and worked the herd, you'd be lucky if you ended up with enough hands for a branding crew.

Mike Logan would be in the keeper cut.

Mike is a bit embarrassed when he is referred to as a cowboy poet because he doesn't follow a cow around for a living. The western landscape is overflowing with folks who, although they may (or may not) be top hands, wouldn't know an iamb from an anapest if they had one on the end of a thirty-foot lariat.

Mike knows. His meter is as tight as the top wire on a new bull pasture fence. His rhyme is not only on target, but a bullseye every time. In addition to all this, he is a master story teller.

Enough said. Enjoy his writing.

Wally McRae

Introduction

The title poem for this book of verse was not, in any way, meant to be a factual account of what happened in Charlie Russell's great painting, *Bronc To Breakfast.* Knowing his penchant for story telling, he was also a fine poet when the mood seized him; I just wanted to make up a story about that picture that I thought Charlie might have enjoyed. *Christmas At The Line Camp*, although it doesn't mention Charlie, was written about another of my favorite Russell paintings.

A word or two of explanation; galluses in *Bronc To Breakfast* means suspenders. That's just what they call them in Kansas and Oklahoma where I grew up. The word "Stand" in *B Movie Badman* comes from the fact that road agents commonly greeted their victims by shouting, "Stand and deliver." There may be a few other terms that will be hard to sort out, but I hope they won't throw you too far off the trail.

Some special "thank you's."

First, to Mike Korn who not only did the fine illustrations, but suggested the title for the book. I think he probably just got tired of hearing me mutter as I tried to figure a way around calling it a book of cowboy poetry. As you'll see, a lot of my poems are not "cowboy" in the strictest sense of the word.

To Wally McRae for writing the foreword. If Wally is not the World All Around Champion Cowboy Poet, you're going to have to wear out a lot of horseflesh trying to find one.

To Gwen Petersen for her zest, enthusiasm and love of words. Without Gwen's seemingly boundless energy, skill and perseverance, there probably would never have been a Montana Cowboy Poetry Gathering.

Thanks, also, to old friends who just talk the way they talk. A lot of the ideas for my poems come from just "sittin' around shootin' the breeze" after a day of branding or shipping or riding on a cattle drive.

If these poems smell like cookfires and coffee then I'm happy. I hope sometime I can sit around your fire and hear a few of your stories.

Mike Logan
Helena, Montana 1988

Contents

Bronc To Breakfast

Dobie rode a bronc to breakfast.
That cayuse was plumb green.
He fed ol' Dobe some biscuits
Still in the fire, I mean.

The camp cook wasn't none too pleased
When Dobe went in the fire.
That bronc spilled all the coffee;
Stomped the bacon in the mire.

Now, Dobe was some preoccupied
That biscuit dough was hot
And the lid from that dutch oven
In his galluses was caught.

Them galluses plumb held that lid,
Three coals was caught inside
And ever' passin' second
Burned 'em deeper in Dobe's hide.

I've been to lots o' brandin's
But this one took the cake,
No matter how he jumped or stomped
Ol' Dobie shore did bake.

Now, Dobe, he finally shed that lid,
His chest was smokin' some
When that bronc that he rode in on
For another pass did come.

That hoss was stompin' bedrolls
And kickin' ropes and hats
And, passin', he just plants a kick
In ol' Dobe's smokin' slats.

Ol' Dobe sits back down in them coals.
His day ain't startin' right.
When he comes up for the second time
He comes up on the fight.

He grabs an ol' black fryin' pan
And whales that bronco's head.
That hoss went down so sudden
We was certain he was dead.

Now, Dobie he just stood there
Black skillet in his hand
And waited 'til that bangtail
Shook hisself and tried to stand.

With his vest and shirt still smokin'
Dobie swung up on his back,
Leaned forward with that fryin' pan
And gave him one more whack.

That bronco's knees, was wobblin'
But Dobie had the cure
He showed that bay just who was boss
And that was certain sure.

It turns out, with a fryin' pan,
Ol' Dobie was a champ.
A rhythm was developin'
As they tore out of camp.

He'd thump that hoss a time or two
Then spur him stem to stern
And then that cast iron skillet
Would get another turn.

That broomtail, he lines out to run.
He knew he'd lost the fight.
We raised a cheer for Dobie
As they flew out of sight.

When he rode back that mornin',
To change his shirt and vest,
A circle red and three dots
Was branded on Dobe's chest.

We called him Circle Three Dot
And he made that mark his brand.
A heap o' critters wore it,
'Fore he quit this big skied land.

Dobe's ride became a legend
In the hist'ry of the west.
And ol' Charlie Russell's paintin'
Prob'ly told the story best.

He rode a bronc to breakfast
But long after ol' Dobe died
They told of Circle Three Dot
And his famous mornin' ride.

Unsaddle David's Sorrel

Unsaddle David's sorrel
He'll ride no more these hills.
He's gone to greener pastures
Where ponies take no spills.

Unsaddle David's sorrel
And lead him to the stall.
Hang up that old gray battered hat
His spurs and ropes and all.

Unsaddle David's sorrel
And pitch him down some hay.
The world holds better memories
'Cause David rode this way.

Beef All Comes From Cellophanes

If milk all comes from cartons
And pickles come from jars
Then green beans sprout from labeled cans
And chocolate comes from bars.

If 'taters come from plastic bags
And cheese from slices neat
Then eggs all come from styrofoams
And juice from bottles sweet.

If shoes all come from boxes
And flour, it grows in sacks
Then beef all comes from cellophanes
And wool shirts come from racks.

Now if beef all comes from cellophanes,
And we all know that's true,
Then I wish somebody'd tell me,
What the hell do ranchers do?

He Always Rode Good Horses

(Rememberin' a Horseman)

"He always rode good horses."
"He did that, fer a fact."
"And he always grained 'em good, with oats,
Before he put 'em back."

"He always had a special way.
His horses really walked."
"His horses did 'most ever'thing,
Though none I knew of talked."

"I never saw him rough with one."
"He didn't need to be.
They seemed to understand him.
It was somethin' just to see."

"He always favored sorrels
And he seemed to like a bay.
And you 'member that good roan horse
He was ridin' that last day."

"Feller spends his life ahorseback,
Ain't so bad a way to go.
They were turnin' back a brindle steer
And hit that badger hole."

"Spill broke his neck as quick as that.
We had to shoot the roan.
Still, he went down doin' what he liked
And what he'd always known."

"He's checkin' Heaven's horse herd, now,
I guess we shouldn't grieve.
'Cause if Heaven lacks good horseflesh,
Hell, he'll prob'ly up and leave!!!"

The Song Of Spring

I heard the song of spring, last night.
It began like some ancient rune.
Old as life itself, it was,
And I recognized the tune.

I heard the wild geese sing, last night,
Far up where they always fly.
A lovely high skied nocturne, they sang,
Winging north in a velvet sky.

I heard the moonsinger howl, last night,
A ballad he'd learned to croon,
Months before on a snowswept ridge,
Silhouetted on the hunger moon.

I heard the creek break loose, last night,
From its hoary armoured bond.
A glorious free voiced chant it raised
As it poured from the frozen pond.

I heard the wind god, too, last night,
His primordial wind song blow
On his trumpet huge the warm soft notes
That drove away the snow.

All these things I heard, last night,
And they formed an ancient rune.
Old as life itself, it was,
And I rejoiced to hear the tune.

Brands

Me an' Slim was movin' heifers
Down Highway 33.
When this Cadillac with New York plates
Pulls up beside o' me.

The lady driver, she leans out
An' waves to me an' him.
Then purty soon she's drivin' 'long
An' talkin' with ol' Slim.

She asks 'im 'bout the cowboy life
An' 'bout his hoss an' such.
An' why them bulls is wearin' stars.
It's plain she don't know much.

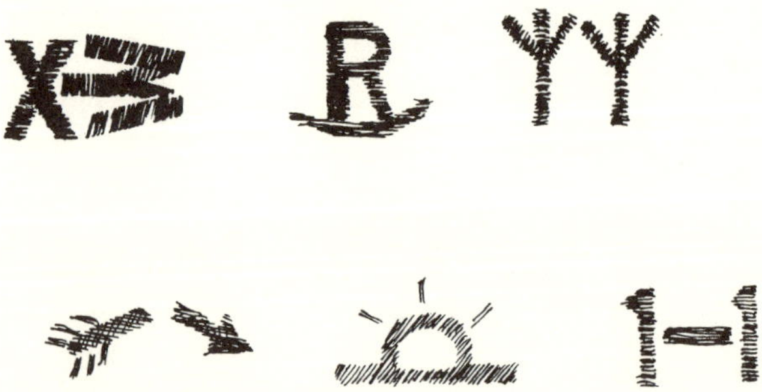

"Well, Ma'am, them stars is brands," Slim says.
"They tell who owns the cow."
She asks him, "Are there many brands?"
That lady's done it now!

Ol' Slim don't usu'lly talk too much,
But he gets plumb wound up!
Ya' get 'im talkin' cattle brands
He's eager as a pup!

"Why, Ma'am, you bet!! There's quite a few!!"
Ol' Slim builds to the task.
"Could you just name a few of them?"
I hear that lady ask.

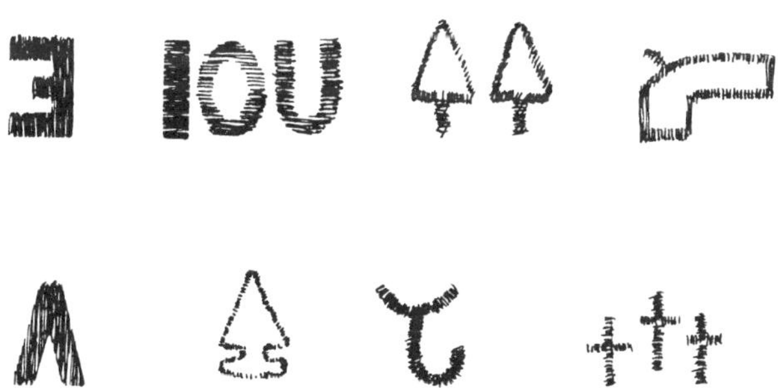

"Shoot, Ma'am, I'd be right happy to!"
He takes a mighty breath.
That lady's in grave danger
O' plumb bein' talked to death!

Ol' Slim, he starts off kind a' slow
Then steams right on ahead.
An' best as I can recollect
These brands is ones he said.

"There's Broken Hearts and Lazy K's
An' Muleshoes an' Walkin' A's.
There's Runnin' W's, Tumblin' T's
An' Bar B Q's an' Di'mond 3's.

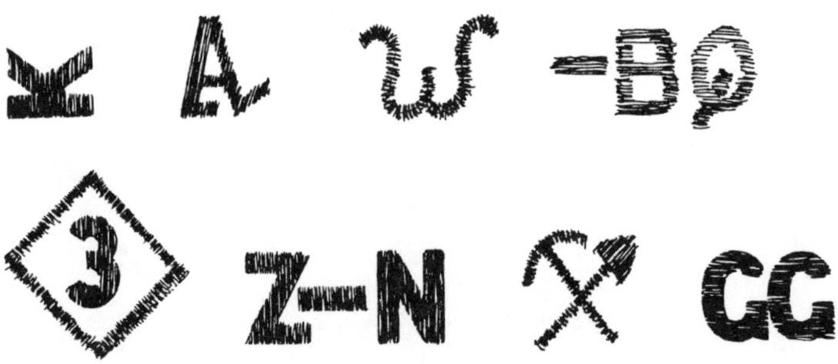

There's X Bar M's an' Rockin' R's
An' Turkey Tracks an' Circle Stars.
There's Y Bar 5's, an' Rafter P's
An' Triangles an' Slash N C's.

There's Broken Arrows, Risin' Suns
An' Tomahawks an' 1 Bar 1's.
There's Quarter Moons an' Backward E's
An' I O U's an' Twin Pine Trees.

There's Six Shooters an' Z Bar N's
An' Question Marks an' Number 10's.
There's Pick and Shovels, Double G's
An' Quarter Circle Crazy B's.

There's Candlesticks an' Open A's
An' Arrowheads an' Hangin' J's.
There's Anchors an' a Triple Cross
An' even some shaped like a Hoss.

There's Pitchers, Teapots an' there's Cups.
An' Wineglasses an' 7 Ups.
There's Cloverleafs an' Mission Bells
An' Eyeglasses an' Schoolboy L's.

There's Top Hats an' there's Buttonhooks
An' lots that's hard to read in books.
There's Box Fs an' the 4 T 4
An', by gum, Ma'am, there's plenty more."

Ol' Slim he's soundin' windbroke
His breath's a comin' rough.
His face's turnin' beet red.
This namin' brands is tough!!

"You mean you haven't named them all?"
That lady cain't but stare.
"Why, I ain't hardly started, Ma'am.
I just run out o' air!"

The Devil An' Ol' Billie Bob

Ol' Billie Bob is plumb confused.
He'd be the first to tell.
He started for them Pearly Gates,
But finds hisself in Hell.

The Devil stands a fumin'
As ol' Billie Bob comes down.
He's breathin' smoke an' red hot fire
An' wearin' a awful frown!

He says, "Just where you headed, Hoss?"
Ol' Billie Bob don't know.
He's discombobulated some
'Bout where he's s'posed to go.

"I saw you try that up trail, Bill."
He flicks his three forked tail.
An' Billie Bob knows where he is.
Them Okies calls it "Hail!"

Billie Bob's a Okie cowboy
Used to summers on them plains.
He tells Ol' Lucifer right off
"Don't take no special pains!"

"I know right where I am, now,
An' I know you set the rule,
But cain't you turn the heat up?
'Hail' seems to me some cool!!"

Ol' Satan he steps back some
An' cracks that awful whip.
His helpers stoke Hell's pit some more.
Billie's teet'rn' on the lip.

"Well, shoot, now that's some better!"
He looks down that fiery hole.
"But you s'pose it's askin' too much
To add a bit more coal?"

"I don't mean to be complainin'
But this thing o' bein' cold,
If I've got to spend eternity,
Could get to be plumb old!"

Ol' Nick he loads them fire pits
'Til they're burnin' hotter'n, well,
I guess you'd say he loads 'em
'Til they're burnin' hotter 'n Hell!

Ol' Billie Bob's relaxin' some.
That furnace works real good.
He volunteers to help them boys
A pitchin' on more wood.

Ol' Mister Devil's sweatin', now.
He's too hot, don't you see.
He decides to send ol' Billie Bob
Back where he used to be.

But Billie Bob don't want to go!
The tempa'ture's just right!
"Hail" feels just like a breath o' spring
On a Oklahoma night!!

He says, "I'll head your furnace crew,
If you'll just let me stay.
Shoot, I'll even put in overtime
If you'll do things my way!!"

"I'll need some men that's used to heat
An' won't their duties shirk!
Just give me Texas cowhands.
I know they'll like the work."

But if you wanta feel real heat
Just come back up with me
It's summer on them Okie plains
An' hot, I guarantee!"

"Why, Beelzebub, I've seed that heat
Plumb melt whole mountains down.
That's why us Okie cowboys
Always works on near flat ground!"

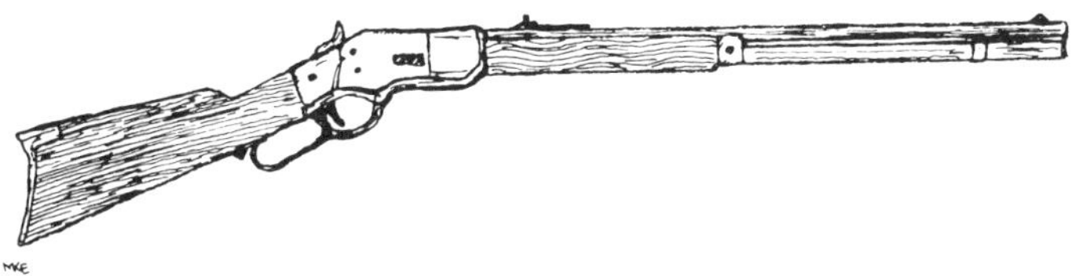

Ol' Satan says it's comf'terble
For him, down there in Hell.
At least it was 'fore Billie Bob
Got things fired up so well!

An' these days, on the gates of Hell,
Is burned this sign, discreet
"NO OKLAHOMA COWBOYS.
SEND THEM OKIES TO ST. PETE."

If the devil gets a hard case, now
That needs to roast real good.
He just thinks of Oklahoma
And he saves his coal and wood.

'Cause when ol' Nick needs real heat
Or true brimstone aroma.
Why, he knows to send them bad ones
All up to Oklahoma!!

Ol' Billie Bob, he's back, now.
I guess that tells my tale
Why there ain't no Okie cowboys
Coolin' off down there in "Hail!!"

Shootist

A shootist who holstered his gun
Just after a shootout he'd won
Shot himself in the lip
And twice in the hip
When his big Colt revolver he spun.

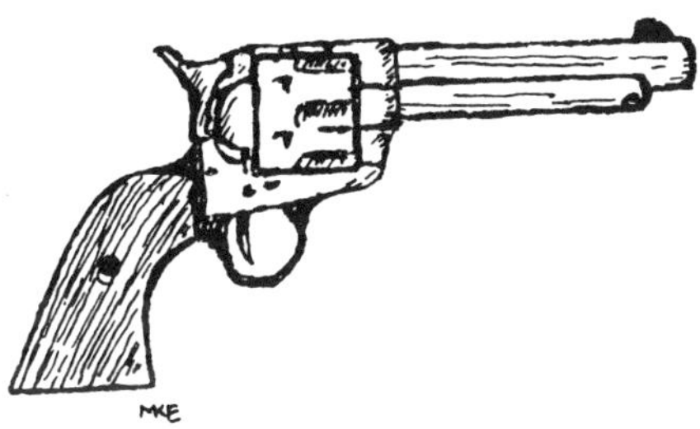

Retired

An old cowboy named Billie Bob Crocker
Retired to just sit in his rocker.
But his wife was a nag,
Made retirement a drag,
So, he traded her in for a cocker.

Ranch Girls

"Movin' cows is man's work!,"
I heard one young buck say.
But Evelyn covered twice the ground
He covered in a day.

"A female don't know heelin' calves!",
He growled, as his loop missed.
But Valerie shades him three to one.
He swore he'd sprained his wrist.

"I'd like to see one drive a team!",
He crowed for all to hear.
But Cherie raked more hay, one week,
Than he did that whole year.

"No girl can keep up on the trail!",
He'd shout, as off he'd ride.
But Gayle came out so far ahead,
We thought his horse had died.

He knows about the ranch girls, now.
How hard they work, and long.
And all those things he'd known for sure
Turned out to be dead wrong!!

Hoof Beats

Hoof beats, I hear hoof beats
In the Southeast Kansas dawn
And the sound brings back my memories
Of horses now long gone.

In my mind, I hear Brown Betty.
I can tell her quick stepped pace
And I know Dad's talkin' to her
As she flies with hobbled grace.

There are more remembered hoof beats,
Movin' fast to beat the clock,
And they conjure old familiar names
Like Ginger, Pete and Doc.

I hear other horses trottin'
On those racetracks of my mind
And the men who trained and loved them
Were a breed now hard to find.

They'd not have said they loved them,
"I just like to see 'em go."
Or, "All I want's the money!"
But you knew it wasn't so.

Hoof beats, I hear hoof beats
In the dew moist Kansas air
And I love to hear those hoof beats
'Cause I know my Dad is there.

The Sundown Team

A straining hitch of muscled roans
High stepped through new mown hay
To draw a dump rake's spring steel claws
Toward the close of day.

As sundown neared, the prancing team
Made one more pass and turned
For home and barn and cool sweet oats
And rest they'd richly earned.

Behind them, gray green windrows
Of work, already done,
Formed graceful curving grass snakes
Awaiting next day's sun.

And waves of evening's fading light
Poured down a golden stream
That gently washed the new made stacks
And bathed the sundown team.

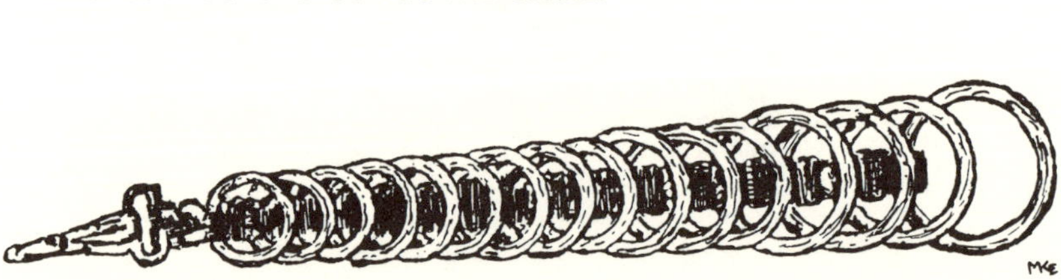

An Ancient Beaverslide

Alone, it stood,
All made of wood,
Hip deep in drifted snow.
Of lodgepole pines
And jutting tines,
Its ribs all seemed to show.

In bygone times
And gentler climes,
It used to stack wild hay.
But nature's rage
And ripe old age
Had placed it there to stay.

Gray arms held high
To touch the sky,
It seemed some fossiled beast
That rose to fight,
To claw and bite
And froze there, facing east.

Its weathered bones
Seemed turned to stones
That, long since, petrified.
It was, in fact,
Though broken backed,
An ancient beaverslide.

Dawn

Dawn comes on velvet tiptoes
To shade the eastern skies.
She lifts rose colored fingertips
And bids the sun to rise.

This soft eyed golden goddess
Steals mountains from the night,
Unfurls her glowing banners
And brings the gift of light.

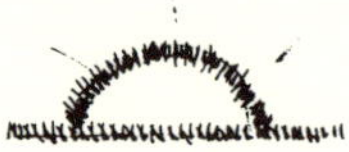

Sun Dagger

Oh, ancient Anasazi man,
Crouched there beside your three stoned shrine,
What wondrous spark first touched your artist's eye
And taught your hand to spiral that design?

Oh, shadowed Anasazi ghost,
Who watched the sun's white dagger shine,
Did some old god the heavens' secrets show
Or did your thoughts make you yourself divine?

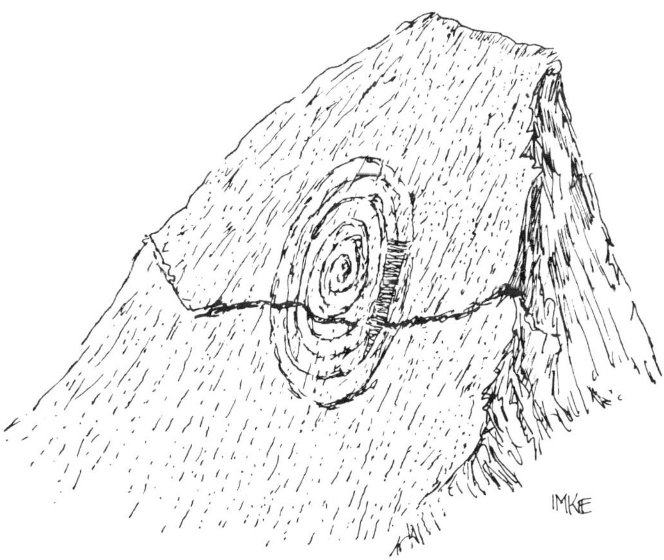

The Wolf Creek Stage

The Wolf Creek stage was runnin' late
An' Red was some put out.
He cussed the road, the dust 'n heat,
But most he cussed Ben Stout.

Now Ben, he ran the stage line
An' Red, he drove the teams.
He'd drove that coach for five long years,
Not once been late, it seems.

But that day Ben was plumb in Dutch
An' Red was on the fight.
He'd had to wait for Ben's wife
An' she weren't trav'lin' light.

With two big trunks of dresses
An' hatboxes galore
She's loaded down the whole stagetop
An' then sent Ben for more.

Red watches all them goin's on.
Departure time's long past.
The strongbox ain't been loaded yet.
His temper's losin' fast.

When Ben Stout finally seats his wife
An' passes up the gold,
Ol' Red's quit foamin' at the bit.
His stare has turned plumb cold.

He snakes out his ol' bull whip
An' gives a rebel yell.
Them teams is pullin' out o' town
Like bats a fleein' Hell.

His hosses runnin' flat out,
Red tries to make up time.
He knows North Hill is comin' up
An' it's a two mile climb.

Now even though he's runnin' late
Red also knows the road.
His teams is lathered up some
'Cause they're pullin' quite a load.

Besides Ben's wife and baggage
Two drummers paid their fares.
Red knows one peddles whiskey
And the other sells housewares.

A third man's wearin' batwings.
His saddle's on the back.
An' ridin' shotgun, up with Red,
Is tough ol' James J. Mack.

So when they hit that up grade
Red slows 'em to a walk.
He starts to lose his mad on
As him and James J. talk.

Red hands James J. them ribbons
An', tellin' some new joke,
He reaches for the makin's
To build 'em each a smoke.

Right then he sees that badman
A standin' by the way,
His sawed off Greener shotgun
Coverin' Red an' ol' James J.

I've told, already, how ol' Red
Ain't never once been late.
He also ain't been held up,
Another thing he'd hate.

James J., he spots that bandit, too.
His ma ain't raised no fool.
He whoas that stage real easy
Then he sits there calm and cool.

That road agent, he speaks real soft.
The Greener tells the tale.
"Just ease me down that strongbox, boys
An' don't forget that mail."

"An' holler to them passengers
To step down nice an' slow!
My partner wants their valuables.
He'll want yours, too, you know."

Sure 'nuff another masked man
Steps to the stagecoach door.
Ol' James J. does just what he's told,
But Red, he's gettin' sore.

He starts to pitch down hatboxes
An' trunks an' saddles, too.
That baddy with the shotgun asks
Just what he's tryin' to do.

Ol' Red, he snaps, "I'm helpin'!!"
As them passengers step out.
Them dress trunks bust wide open
An' Ben's wife begins to shout!

"Red, you great big lummox!
You're doing that for spite!"
Them robbers never made no plans
To referee no fight!"

"Nel," Red says, "that hurts me,
You thinkin' such a thing!"
He picks up three more hatboxes
An' gives 'em each a fling.

Nel sees her best new bonnets
All pitched down in the dust,
Her dresses trampled underfoot,
She's just about to bust!

Them teams is gettin' restless.
They're pawin' at the dirt,
But Nel Stout's really mad now,
She don't care who gets hurt.

"Red," she shouts, "I'll get you!"
An' she starts to climb up top.
It was then that both them bandits
Starts a tellin' her to stop.

The one that holds the Greener
Ain't speakin' soft no more.
An' to get back their attention
He fires straight up, with a roar!

Ol' Red just draws an' shoots 'im,
Right between them cold blue eyes.
An' you might say that his partner
Just died from plain surprise.

You see, ol' James J. cut him down
While he was watchin' Red.
In less time than it takes to tell,
Them outlaws, both, was dead.

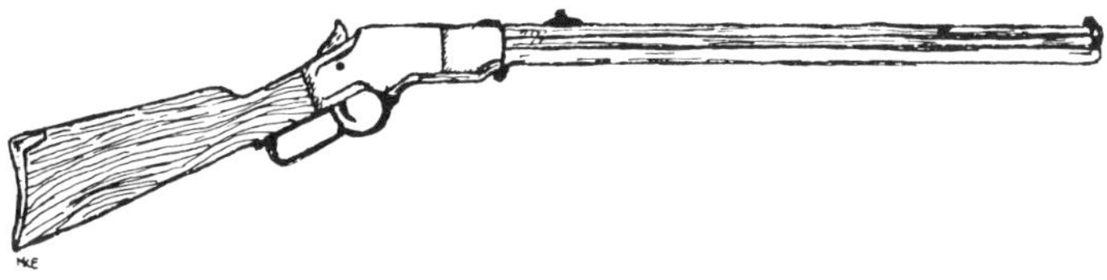

But Red, he still ain't happy.
He's got this one track mind.
"Just pitch 'em off the road, boys.
We're runnin' some behind!"

"We'll send somebody back for them.
We got no time to spare.
An', Nel, you quit that bawlin'
An' get on down from there!"

"Just gather up them dresses
An' get 'em put away.
An' hurry with them bonnets,
'Cause we ain't got all day!"

When ever'thing's reloaded
An' Red's all set to go
He starts them teams uphill again,
Still movin' nice and slow.

But when they top that North Hill
There's drivin' to be done.
Red's whip commences talkin'
An' them hosses starts to run.

In two jumps them ol' ponies
Is all snorty an' wild eyed.
Ol' Red ain't holdin' back none
An' it's some scary ride.

You see, the north side's steeper
An' downhill ain't no fun.
Them teams is just a tryin'
That stagecoach to outrun.

They hit the flats a' tearin',
Throwin' dust up to the sky.
Ol' Red's a pushin' on them reins.
The sage is flyin' by.

An' Wolf Creek Canyon's up ahead
That road's all hairpin curve.
To drive it at a dead run
Takes lots o' skill an' nerve.

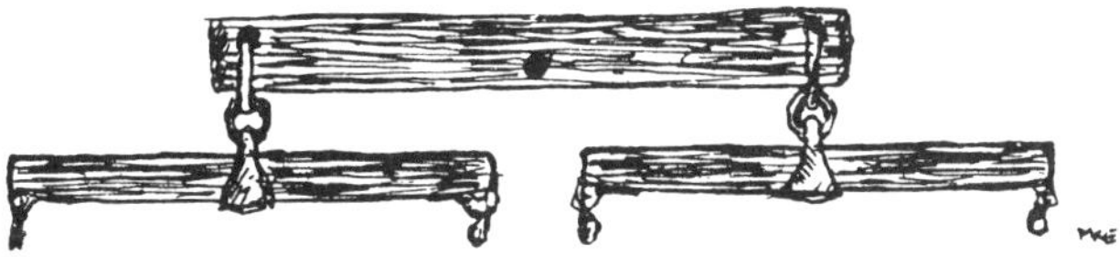

Red two wheels all them hairpins,
An' with no hills to climb,
When he thunders into Wolf Creek,
He's runnin' right on time.

His teams is blowin' mighty hard,
The baggage ain't on straight,
Ol' James J.'s got a death grip,
But Red, still ain't been late.

Nel never rode with Red no more
When she was headed east
An' the Wolf Creek Stage weren't once held up,
Not successfully at least.

That's purt' near all my story
About that long gone stage.
How two men who tried to rob it
Never lived to see old age.

They planted them two outlaws
High up on ol' North Hill.
They called the place Road Agent Rock.
I guess they always will.

But when the moon's a risin'
An' the north wind's whippin' 'round,
Men tell o' hearin' shotguns
An' another wilder sound.

They say they hear a bullwhip
An' the screech o' ironbound wheels
An' the sound o' hosses runnin'
Like the devil's on their heels.

An' you know ol' Red's a drivin',
His ghost teams all wild eyed,
On a phantom stage to Wolf Creek
With ol' James J. by his side.

A Puncher's String

Bill Burnett, he was the foreman
For the old time D H S
An' his boss, ol' Granville Stuart,
Had stirred up quite a mess.

Bill stomped into the bunkhouse.
On the prod, you understand.
He was a Texas puncher
An' a sure 'nuff top cowhand.

Well, he gathers up his plunder
An' he saddles his own hoss.
Then he lopes up to the main house
An' asks to see the boss.

"I'd like to draw my time, Boss,
An' I'll be on my way."
"Aw, Bill, now what's the matter?"
"You sold my little bay."

"But, I sold 'im to my partner
An' the hoss belonged to me.
He needed a good trav'ler
For his business, don't you see?"

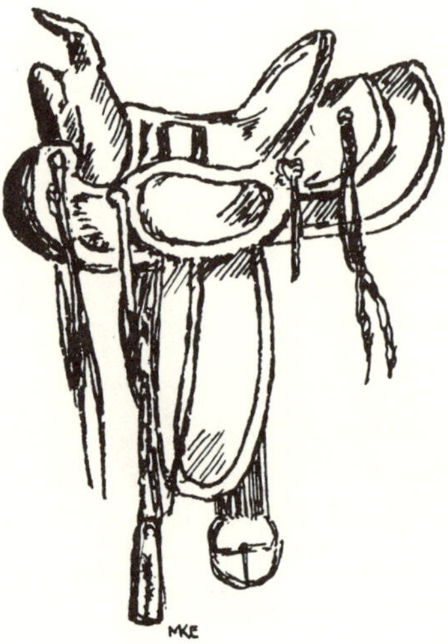

"Well, Boss, you never asked me.
That bay's from my own string.
I know the outfit owns him,
But that don't mean a thing."

"You never sell a puncher's hoss
Without you ask him first.
And, Boss, you should 'a knowed it
And that's what hurt the worst."

"Well, Bill, I didn't know it.
I'd sure like to have you stay.
If you don't I'll understand, though,
And we'll go and get your pay."

Bill didn't care if Granville
Was the boss an' ever'thing.
Nobody sold a pony
From a Texas cowboy's string.

You didn't even loan one
Not even to the boss,
At least without permission
From the man who rode the hoss.

"Now, Boss, if you'd a asked me
I'd sure a said 'You bet!!'
But to sell 'im without askin'
Well, that I cain't forget."

"The man who owns a cayuse
Can sell 'im, that's his right.
But not to tell the cowpoke,
Well, that just ain't polite!"

Ol' Granville, he apologized
So Bill decides to stay
An' Stuart found his partner
An' bought back the little bay.

An old puncher, E. C. Abbott,
Most folks called 'im Teddy Blue,
Was the one who told this story
An' he said that it was true.

He said ranchers from Montana
Had to learn a thing or two
'Bout Texicans 'n ponies,
What they would an' wouldn't do.

Teddy said them Texas punchers
Who brought cattle to this range
Was touchy 'bout their hosses
An' they weren't about to change.

That old sayin' 'bout not teachin'
An old dog a new trick
Weren't meant for Granville Stuart
'Cause that lesson sure did stick.

Unless he asked the cowboy first,
No matter what he'd bring,
Stuart never sold a cowhorse
From another puncher's string.

Ode To LAX

(L.A. International Airport)

Noise,
People noise,
Assaults my ailing ears.
Bumped and jostled,
L. A. International Airported,
Attacked by monotoned announcings,
I think on other things.

I think on rams along the ridgeline.
I think on bulls along the Yellowstone.

Smog,
People smog,
Insults my suffering nose.
Belched and billowed,
L. A. high speed freewayed,
Stung by countless sulfured smokescreens,
I think on other things.

I think on wildflowers at the cow camp.
I think on breezes down the Great Divide.

Heat,
People heat,
Embroils my throbbing head.
Burned and blistered,
L. A. Southern Californiaed,
Driven frantic by the steamings,
I think on other things.

I think on cutthroat in the Beartooth.
I think on glaciers in the sky.

I think on mountains in the sunshine.
I think on snowfall in the rimrocks.

I think on home.

Autumn

Autumn sees the leaves dance
And flaunt their colors bold.
A gilt edged lovely falling time,
It turns the earth to gold.

Autumn ends the harvest
And breathes old thanks filled tunes.
A fruitful swollen storing time,
It hangs huge yellow moons.

Autumn dresses morning
In muted gray fog coats.
A ghostly muffled quiet time,
It whispers silvered notes.

Autumn guides the waterfowl
Down old ancestral ways.
A peaceful far voiced flying time,
It brings on shortened days.

Autumn chants a death song
That signals winter's near.
A gentle red brown dying time,
It tapers off the year.

Evening

Evening mounts a dark horse
And lopes, when day is done,
Across deep purple mountains
Toward a dying sun.

A silent, shadowed drover,
He herds the last stray light,
Eludes the growing darkness
And rides the edge of night.

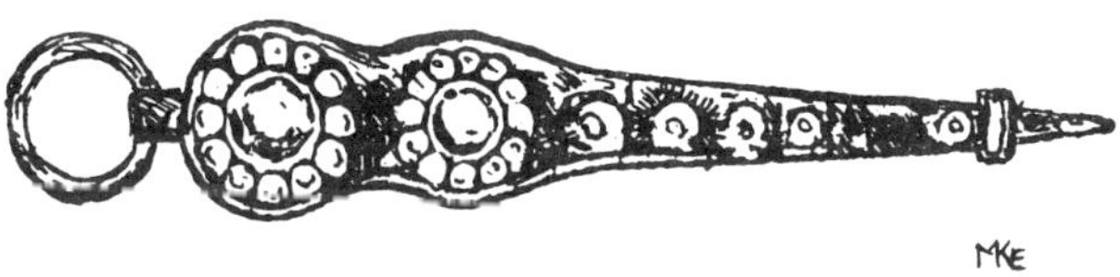

B Movie Badman

He rode a blaze faced sorrel
With four white stocking feet.
His hat and all his clothes were black,
His gunbelt, oiled and neat.

He sat an inlaid saddle.
The silver really shone.
His vest bore brilliant conchos.
His pistol grips were bone.

He wore a jet black string tie,
With white shirt, starched and clean.
His boots were hand tooled leather.
His eyes flashed dark and mean.

He robbed the morning stagecoach
With big black Colt in hand.
His voice was deep and resolute.
His order was to "Stand."

He covered up his handsome face
With his bandana red.
He pulled it down, rode back to town
And not one word was said.

I rode a darkened movie seat
And almost lost my mind.
Why were the victims, on the stage,
So suddenly struck blind?

"Just look. He's wearing all black clothes.
His vest and saddle shine.
His sorrel horse has four white feet."
No eyes could see but mine.

The marshals always got their man.
I never could see why.
To get caught by those good guys
Badmen really had to try.

The hero wore a white hat tall
To cover up his head.
It seemed, to me, a signal that
Between his ears was dead.

He used that part so little that
I thought he sure was dumb.
What would he ever do for help
If I were not to come?

I warned those helpless lawmen
Every Saturday afternoon.
They never seemed to hear me.
They'd just play another tune.

"You've got to watch his riggin'
And listen when he talks.
You've got to study horses
And the way a badman walks."

By the end of every matinee
When I walked out the door
I knew that come next weekend
I'd buy one ticket more.

I had to ride that movie seat
And see how well I'd taught
He'd rob the morning stage again,
And never once get caught.

I don't know just how old I was
Before I finally learned,
It was me he stuck up weekly
And my nickels that he earned.

Christmas At The Line Camp

It's Christmas at the line camp
All blizzardy an' cold.
Me n' Jake's fresh out o' makins'.
Our own comp'ny's gettin' old.

My bay hoss, he's plumb off his feed.
The new ax handle's broke.
Man, I'd plumb give my saddle
If I just had a smoke.

A blizzard hit on Christmas Eve.
Ol' Jake's shore feelin' low.
The storm don't really matter much.
There ain't no place t' go.

The blizzard's fin'lly liftin' some.
The world's all froze n' blue.
The line camp's wearin' a gloomy face.
I reckon we are too.

Then ringin' down the South Fork Trail,
As clear as any bell,
"Hallooo the camp!! Ya' in there, Slim?
Okay to light a spell?"

It's Bud n' Shorty ridin' up
From down at the Bar N.
Somehow it don't much matter when
It starts to snow again.

"Well, shore, boys, yore plumb welcome!!
Step down an' come on in!!"
Ol' Bud hands me the makin's
A wearin' this big ol' grin.

"Well, Shorty shot a' antelope
A comin' 'crost the flat.
We thought ya'd like some fresh meat!!
An' this buck's prime an' fat!"

"Why, he'll be better 'n bacon.
He'll make some Christmas feast!"
The storm's a buildin' outside.
Ain't fit fer man n'r beast.

But me 'n' Bud slip out again
An' cut a little pine.
We set it in the window
An' it shore looks mighty fine.

While Jake's a cookin' pronghorn steaks
An' Shorty's fixin' spuds,
We start t' decorate the tree
With stuff o' mine an' Bud's.

I'm shapin' danglin' snowmen
From ol' Bull Durham sacks
An' Bud, he's usin' can lids
An' melted candle wax.

When Christmas dinner's ready
We're finished with the tree.
Bud's silver spur's a twinklin' star.
An' it's some sight to see.

Them pronghorn steaks is mighty fine.
Jake even baked a pie.
We loose our belts a notch 'r two
An' lean back with a sigh.

An' after that fine dinner
We build ourselves some smokes.
We couldn't a' been no richer
With millions in our pokes.

Then Jake gets out his bible
With its cover smooth an' worn
An' he reads that age old story
Of the day when Christ was born.

Jake's wrinkled face's wind burned.
His forelock's white as snow.
Looks like some old time angel
In that lantern's golden glow.

He tells how baby Jesus
With no place else to go
Is born among cow critters
In that stable long ago.

An' how the star of Bethlehem
Shines bright for them three kings
An' leads 'em to the Christ child
With all the gifts each brings.

An' sittin' in that line shack
A hearin' that Christmas tale
We think o' other pardners
We've knowed along life's trail.

T' each we send a silent wish
For Yuletide peace and cheer
An' goodwill on the range lands
Through all the comin' year.

Now, when I think o' Christmases
An' which ones was the best,
That Christmas at the line camp
Stands out from all the rest.

'Cause, pards, the Christmas spirit
Ain't what you get 'r give.
Friends 'n' family's what makes Christmas,
No matter where you live.

Ol' Cooky

Now, Ol' Cooky was some ugly
An' he surely weren't no rose.
If you lost him in a stampede
You could find him with your nose.

Cooky wasn't scared of water.
Shoot, he used it ever' day
Makin' coffee, beans and biscuits,
But wash in it? No way!!!

Now, I ain't faultin' Cooky.
He could sure 'nuff rustle grub.
But he'd get just plain insulted
At the mention of a tub.

Cooky's apple pie was heaven.
It just seemed some angel's blend.
Punchers purt' near fought for seconds,
But they always ate upwind.

Cooky's wagon, it was spotless.
Plates and cups was shiny clean.
But you just mention bathin'
An' Ol' Cooky'd get plumb mean.

You really cain't blame Cooky.
He only had one shirt.
We never knowed which parts was cloth
An' which parts grease and dirt.

I roped a skunk for Cooky once.
Just did it for a joke!!
When I drug him up to Cooky,
Well, I thought that skunk'd choke.

We lost Ol' Cooky that year.
At a crossin' on the Platte.
Chuckwagon tipped in midstream.
We only found his hat.

Ol' Cooky never learned to swim.
A fact, too late found out.
'Course, I always thought if watered right
Ol' Cooky'd prob'ly sprout.

He's likely makin' pine trees, now,
With needles long and green.
He lived his life in one old shirt,
But he met his Maker clean.

PHOTO/MIKE LOGAN

Mike Korn is one of that rare breed of cat, called a folklorist, without whose efforts a lot of the old-time cowboy poems and songs might have slipped into oblivion. The folklorist for the state of Montana, he is also an accomplished writer, photographer, musician, speaker, leather worker, cowhand and, of course, illustrator.

One of the original planners of both the National Cowboy Poetry Gathering in Elko, Nevada, and the Montana Cowboy Poetry Gathering in Big Timber, Mike could safely be called a Renaissance man.

He lives near Helena with his wife, Jane, and twin daughters, Lauren and Alicia.